Buddhist Prayer for Healing

Just as the soft rains fill the streams,
pour into the rivers, and join together in the oceans,
so may the power of every moment of your goodness
flow forth to awaken and heal all beings–
those here now, those gone before, those yet to come.

The Light is Everywhere
Appalachia Zen Poetry

Victor Depta, Edwina Pendarvis
Timothy Russell, Barbara Sabol,
and Larry Smith

Blair Mountain Press

Bottom Dog Press

Copyright © 2025

Bottom Dog Press / Bird Dog Publishing
PO Box 425 / Huron, OH 44839
http://smithdocs.net
&
Blair Mountain Press
124 East Todd Street
Frankfort, Kentucky 40601
https://blairmtp.net

ISBN
9781947504479

Credits
Edited by Larry Smith & Edwina Pendarvis
Cover Design by Susanna Sharp-Schwacke
Layout and Design by Larry Smith
Art from Shutterstock (copyrighted)

Acknowledgments
The writers here acknowlege the many publications that previously published their work, though the rights remain with the authors.

TABLE OF CONTENTS

Introduction: Every Day Zen	9
Victor Marshall Depta	11
About the Author	11
Statement on Appalachia and Zen	12
When April with Its Sweet Showers	13
A Huge Embrace	13
To Long for the Impossible	14
The Unlocatable Sweet Scent	15
The Lack of Worth	15
Clover	16
Borrowing from Eternity	17
That Which Cannot Be Said	17
Who Could Imagine Time	18
Emptiness	19
Forgoing the World	20
In the Pines, In the Pines	20
The Leaves	21
The Crocuses	21
The Tao	22
Rain Shower	22
The Pond	23
The Light Is Everywhere	24
The Winter Sun	25
Edwina (Eddy) Pendarvis	
About the Author	27
Prose Statement	27
Walking in Beauty	
While We Sleep	31
So "The Song of Songs"	31
Journey	32
How to Enter an Iceberg	33
Connections	
Approaching the Sacred	34
Winter Solstice	35
Quickly	36
Spring/ Summer/ Fall/ Winter	37

Duality
Burial Ground	38
Isleta Pueblo	38
Sculpting the Air	39
Reptilian Brain	40
Something like Enlightenment	41
Mother	41

Duality
Haunting	42
Fragment	42
Fingerprints	43

Barbara Sabol

About the Author	45
Beholding the Mountains: The Poet's "i"	45
Sliding the Boat Back In	47
Return	48
Given Back	49
Haiku	50
Ode to Spring, Peeper	51
Summer Along the Stonycreek	51
Haiku	52
The Wild Wood	53
Haiku	54
Fishing the Stonycreek	54
Haiku	55
Song of Wood	56
The Art of Stacking Wood	57
Waterwheel	57
Kind of Blue	59
Why Our Mothers Warned Us About Playing in the Creek	60
Imperative	60
Haiku	61
Happiness	61
Distant Harvest	62
(Acknowledgments)	63

Timothy J. Russell

About the author	65
Working-Class Zen	66
The Margin for Error	67
Vigilance	68
Even If It's Wrong	69
Steel Mill Ornithology	70
Small Wonder	71
In Loco Citato	72
Jade Plant	74
Pigeon	75
Nothing More, Nothing Less	76
Don't Get Up	76
The Mechanic	77
In Varia Lectio	78
Tim's Haiku	79

Larry Smith

About the Author	81
Everyday Zen: A Statment	82
My Hut	83
Things My Father Taught Me	84
Biking the Allegheny Trail	85
The Letting	87
Crescents	87
Bird Talk	88
At Dusk	88
Learning by Heart	89
Clouds at the End of the Street	89
Sweetness	90
Blackbird	91
Loving Loss	92
Connections	93
Remembrance	93
Monday Morning	94

Every Day Zen

Our Intentions:

It seems that every day our personal lives can become universal. And those moments of union open a quiet deep awareness, a moving revelation of life itself. Those times are what is captured in most art and particularly in zen poems (lower case). The source of such moving presence is as varied as life itself: a candle burning in a humble hut, a dog turning at the sound of a bird, a woman wiping the dirt off her face or yours, sunlight gently resting on a field or lake, or on the hairs of your arm. I find these poems close to nature, to work, to people and their daily lives. They are not unlike the poems of the ancient Zen poets.

Call it tao, zen, mysticism, spirit, grace, it is a humble yet profound sense of duality and presence. Such awareness is what most art and this poetry is all about as you will find here. We welcome you into our home.
Neither a treatise on Zen nor a comprehensive anthology, this gathering of five poets simply intends to present and affirm a vein of writing that is long and strong in our Appalachian writing and culture. Each poet shares his or her story, makes a statement about zen writing from Appalachia, then offers their Appalachia zen poems.
Thanks to the poets of Blair Mountain Press and of Bottom Dog Press for offering to share this work.
Enjoy.
                          - Larry Smith (May 2025)

Victor Marshall Depta

Since we are focusing on Appalachia and Zen, to say that I am a coal-camp hillbilly is appropriate since I was born in the mountains and raised for fifteen years in the coal camps of Logan County, West Virginia, the result of which has been a lifelong hostility towards industrial capitalism, the economic exploitation of miners and the decimation of the environment. The other effect of the mountains is the Pentecostal passion for a spiritually ecstatic experience of God.

Escape from that hillbilly hell-in-paradise is, of course, the military. My four years in the Navy felt like the old-fashioned Grand Tour: Imperial Beach, California; Yokohama and Fukuoka in Japan; and the Florida Keys. I think the U.S. Government lost some money on my tours of duty, but I learned a lot about Zen while in Japan, and I certainly was aesthetically educated by the beauty of the world.

The other escape from poverty in the mountains is education, and I went full-on, ultimately obtaining a PhD in the American Renaissance, especially the Transcendentalism of Whitman, Emerson and Thoreau. And my years in stoned San Francisco were certainly an escape. And then, in 1969 when I was thirty in Pineknob in Raleigh County, West Virginia, I was enlightened by the knowledge that reality is a darkness of the potential creativity of anything, anywhere, particularly of the blue, spikey beauty of a thistle on a scraggly hillside.

The rest is ordinary—raising my daughter, teaching for forty years, writing poems, novels, short stories, mysteries, essays, establishing Blair Mountain Press in 1999—and now the extraordinary opportunity of working with Larry Smith at Bottom Dog Press.

Statement on Appalachia and Zen

If you are fortunate to live in the mountains and have, as most everyone does, discord and dissention in the house, you can walk out the back door and be in the wilderness (You might have to circle the coal tipple to get there). Such was my case, the isolation required for meditation—solitude and silence and beauty. Of course, I'd never heard of Zen, yet in retrospect those times of merely being, empty-headed as any child can be, led me to a susceptibility to the natural world which has never left me. Silence. Nothing.

And I don't know how most people respond to religion, but I was involved in Pentecostal worship all those formative years. I always suspected there was something kind of off with people hollering to the empty air, yet their ecstasy, their suffering and pain, could break my heart and I thought that there must be an answer to suffering. And I found it through Buddhism.

As for Enlightenment itself, I suppose it can come naturally for anyone, but I don't think my experience up in Pineknob in 1969 could have happened without preparation, and I would like to think my nine years of work toward the PhD in literature was as much for enlightenment as it was preparation for teaching. And what was that Enlightenment?

It seemed like a simple, almost ordinary experience —a sudden knowledge of reality as an empty yet anticipatory creation of whatever is material, a darkness out of which all things rise, including light and the earth and us. It was liberation and joy, and it taught me that there is no escape from suffering but through compassion and loving-kindness.

When April with its Sweet Showers
Geoffrey Chaucer
The Canterbury Tales

these are the days
of wild geraniums and bluebells
without a reason but the blithe air
of tulips and irises in the yards
which call forth praise
though if we were imagining a poet
to express our gratitude
that person could not sing as sparrows do
and what a scene
those feathery bundles
those little, chirping riots of eternity

A Huge Embrace
William Blake
Auguries of Innocence
"To see a world in a Grain of Sand
And a Heaven in a Wild Flower—"

what is this thing, eternity
where time isn't there
and nothing is, either
with nowhere to go, or be from
but more like a fog you step out of
and into
one of those white mists
where everything is missing but is
including any meaning whatsoever
but for your knowing
the knowing of emptiness
very peaceable
of what could be a light in darkness
a darkness in the light

where you want to kiss and hug
in a huge embrace
especially the weeds
whimsical in the waste places
in Appalachia

To Long for the Impossible
      Percy Bysshe Shelley
      Adonais LII
      "Life, like a dome of many-colour'd glass,
      Stains the white radiance of Eternity—"

to long for the impossible
would be absurd—
how alter age or talent
or ask for gravity to desist
or for imperishable bliss
but to long for unity
is that not latent in the torso
chest-centered, in what is called the heart
that nowhere ache
and the desire for union
for inseparability, for intercourse
is that not reasonable
unlike the pale complacency of the dead
and in its origins lauded worldwide
wading to and fro
in the arteries, the veins
urgent, necessarily unwise and profligate—
ah, that light where eternity reigns

The Unlocatable Sweet Scent

Buddhists say of the world
it is an emptiness
and we are bound within it
as not being, and wordless
bowed, earth-heavy, like the
peonies and on the fences
as the swags of honeysuckle
and as the thunderstorms
in their gray ropes and curls of clouds—
but similes are not a reality
not the stars in our galaxy
gossamer-white—
no, nothing compares
unlocatable as a sweet scent in May
those expressions of emptiness
where eternity is
all through the day

The Lack of Worth

> Andrew Marvell
> "The Garden"
> "Annihilating all that's made
> To a green thought in a green shade."

in the thought of emptiness
is the tall redtop along the road
thin, slender
delicate in its lack of worth
and the bristlegrass, too
the arc of the seed head
and quiet breath
in the pause where nothing is
the chicory and salsify
and I, also, in an emptiness of bliss

untouched for the moment
the burdock, sticktights, the horseweed
without meaning but being merely
a green habitation
there

Clover

of all the world's events
clover does not signify
or the honeybees
nor do the butterfly weeds
or the butterflies themselves
to be dwelt on
colorful, sweet distractions, indulgences
but truthfully
when the florets in a clover
create an airy, small white blossom
and the gold-and-black barred honeybee
alights fumblingly—
they introduce by such an image
how eternity, diminished in the grass
is illustrated

Borrowing from Eternity

such comfort there is in naming things
as if borrowing from eternity
examples of it
the hummingbirds, the honeysuckle and trumpet vines
that one might think
there was a purpose in consonants and vowels
other than our babbling and common needs
some song or another
the faint voice, again and again
almost perceptible, as the breath is
not quite a mantra
not quite a hymn
but a relief, nonetheless
in the cool, balmy evening
the cicadas' loud, chirring song
and all such sweet reprieves, moment by moment
in our unbelonging

That Which Cannot Be Said
Apophatic Mysticism

there is no doubt that ecstasy was
mystical without names
and the consequences of loving-kindness
were sweet as the lilacs at the gate
as if reality were fresh as the apple blossoms in the
    yard
yet the joy was assailed by history
from Troy to Stalingrad, Carthage to Warsaw,
    Jericho to Aleppo
so, how verify the ineffable with the names of things
those pale companions of emptiness
ephemeral as the clouds
their refulgent edge, their reddened glory at twilight

the hours which tinge the mind also
so we create our metaphors, approximations
melancholy, perhaps, as a train whistle
as though eternity had a sound
wistful, far away in the mountains

Who Could Imagine Time

who could imagine time
a no-thing, really
without the inference of a cloud
a field, the sun and rain
and stones, and everything
and why not the coneflowers
in the fields and waste places
and ironweed, too, and goldenrods
the comfort there—
yet they are timeless, too
since all such things are eternity reified
the mallows along the bank
and the beebalms, fiery red
the gaudy black-eyed susans
and the asters, too
would be there
modestly blue

Emptiness
> *The Heart Sutra*
> "all phenomena in their own
> being are empty"

if there were a name for the other of each thing
it would be a rainbow minus the earth
a corona without the moon
and at dawn
the slightest ripples on a pond
would glitter without a bank
or reeds, or anything
and the self would be
body-less as a bowl
an open window no bird flies through
a door no one walks out of—
they would be white
without a pen or brush
unwritten on
in the emptiness of light

Forgoing the World

I could not, as the Buddhists do
extinguish myself
I could not forgo the lotus on which he rests
his metaphysics minus the pond, the blossoms
pure white, the yellow stamen and pistil
nor the dragonflies
their wings iridescent, tiny rainbows
hovering
where beauty devours itself
where aged men shuffle
where aged women hobble there
circling the blossoms

In the Pines, In the Pines
            Bill Monroe
           In the Pines
     "In the pines, in the pines
     Where the sun never shines
     And we shiver when the cold wind blows—"

the sighing time
so much melancholy
as if one were born to it
in the pines, in the pines—
the wild asters along the path
the last leaves rustling
and the sun
as if strewn underfoot in the autumn leaves
and overhead the geese
the ragged V of them
the crickets, pensive as they chirr
the emptiness in this sweet ache
this sorrow in the wake of eternity

The Leaves
        John Keats
        "To Autumn"

October certainly will do
these sky-blue, windless days
as Keats said about the bees
they think warm days will never cease
and in our reprieve from the cold
are the leaves
languidly discolored, drifting
orange, yellowed, scarlet in their descent
down to us who linger with the weight of time
sighing while leaves unbind themselves of all
    that's green
in their bright unbeing

The Crocuses

they have come back
the lowly ones on the lawns
the crocuses in the barren grass
almost a cliché now for springtime
small enough underfoot, under the widening sky
bluish purple, vividly yellow in their tiny space
to be, almost, vast as eternity
and in the sky, the great queen
enrobed in her entourage of pale blue days
is heralded by the March wind
and perhaps a jonquil or two, trumpeting
a few twigs of forsythia in their chartreuse charm
for her
but mostly the crocuses
the little blossoms, winsome in the cold
in their holiness

The Tao

the leaf shadows are nothing
really
wavering on the sidewalk
insubstantial as thought
as myself
and the sun on my shoulders
in an emptiness walking by
and the breeze, also
and the clouds and the sky

Rain Shower

in the summer heat and humidity
comes the rain
more of a shower, really
and afterwards
the hills are loosed from themselves
and in the mist
unmoored
free from the ordinary
they hover
not hillsides any more
but that nowhere place near the heart
where everything unsaid in life
beautiful and pale white, lingers

The Pond

it is the news disturbs me
and not this first week of November at the pond
the cattails
when the sun reflects a shimmering of themselves
beige and pale green on the water
graceful in their dying
and their renewal, of course, on the stalks
and the barn, too, and the red truck
in the ubiquitous light
radiant of everything illuminating the day
which is not the death of species in the newscasts
or what we read of the far away
the glaciers melting and fires and storms
but the sun
is as much a forever as we could ask for
on this particular day, this pond
and my fondness for the idea of eternity
though a lovely thought
that this day is infinite as a now
that, too, intrudes
when in all that light, rising there in the water
barren of meaning and beautiful
they merely are

The Light Is Everywhere

in an instant
and I would say
being from the mountains
in the pines, in the pines
beautiful in its moment of emptiness
that enlightenment was such
and in conclusion woke me, or anyone
to the light which is everywhere
and easy enough to celebrate it, say
in the resplendence rhododendrons no one will ever see
far back on the mountains
and, too, one Jewish child in the incomprehensible
    smoke
but the light is everywhere in wickedness, in slaughter
—what we do to ourselves is lighted in eternity
and the innocence on a ridge, the greenbriers,
    the thistles
everything is light, death is, and birth
and where but in holiness
but in compassion
almost transparent in the emptiness
is it most bright

The Winter Sun

in the winter sun
suddenly on my walk
was a light-filled joy
as if my eyes misled me
and in and through the trees
everywhere I looked
was radiance
and was gone, then
but for the afterglow
and puzzling as to why I should
(the kindly cynic I tend to be)
have such a happening to
me and how appraise it—
perhaps at my age
as the stories go
it was a light there in the brain
before the end of things
a collapse on the sidewalk
refulgent, into oblivion
but I survived
and the puzzle is
I was far from meditation walking,
bundled against the cold
when eternity overtook me
rushing headlong in its now
and I, slow ploughman
was caught up in it, unaware

Edwina Pendarvis

Walking in Beauty
I was born in Weeksbury (in Floyd County, Kentucky) lucky enough to spend my childhood in the mountains of central Appalachia. By the time I was a year old, we lived In Kopperston (in Wyoming County, WV), and when I was seven, we moved to Wharton (in Boone County, WV), and then when I was nine, we moved to Pikeville, Kentucky, the first place I lived that wasn't a coal camp. I had no idea of the economic inequity and environmental damage of coal mining or the less than benevolent purpose behind the development of coal camps. My friends and I were free to run and play through everybody's backyard and spill over into the creeks and up the hills. We climbed anything we could wrap our arms and legs around, whether trees or clothesline poles. As I remember it, almost every road had a creek or river on one side and a rock cliff or tree-covered incline on the other. The adventurous pleasure of that place and time made me feel the power of the Navajo admonition and prayer to "walk in beauty" and similar sentiments in Taoist descriptions of the "Way" when I came across them as an adult.

To me, the notion of walking in beauty means taking pleasure in the natural world and contributing to its beauty by acting in ways that reflect understanding the world. Darwin's *The Origin of Species*, for example, contributes to walking in beauty by telling us how connected to each other we all are in that environmental factors, such as weather, plants, and animals, create and change each other. In the 20th century, astronomers asserted our connectedness to the cosmos, telling us that we, along with everything around us, are "stardust," composed of remnants of supernovas eons ago. Such theories make me think of all humans as my "cousins." In a way—though I feel it less—other animals, as well as plants and minerals are cousins, too, at least distant cousins. One of my favorite books and movies, *Dersu Uzala,* features a hunter (a native of Siberia, I think), who explains to his friend that a wild boar threatening their safety is a "man," only in a "different shirt." It's important to note that while Taoism emphasizes the ugly elements of war, it doesn't represent the Way as refusing to fight, but as doing so seriously and with compassion when defense of self or others is called for. Fighting to restore unjust disruption of beauty, harmony, and balance can help restore the "Way."

    Contributing to a sense of connectedness with the world is Einstein's recognition of the duality of energy. What we call matter, he said, is simply energy vibrating slowly. I haven't read it yet, but surely *The Tao of Physics*, which focuses on quantum theory, considers the duality of fundamentals, such as light, appear in particle form or in wave form, depending on how they're observed (measured) as another instance of connection—the same basic form of existence expressing itself in different ways.

In a maybe questionable leap, I equate energy with spirit, including the qi or chi associated with Taoism. Given that perspective, the animism of Native American and other religions that regard even apparently inanimate things—such as wind—as spirits is compatible with contemporary science. Elements of both ways of thinking about the universe offer comfort in that they suggest that when we die our body changes into other forms of energy and is still part of the world we loved.

Walking in Beauty

While We Sleep

Salamanders, startled into being,
flicker far away, through the banked fires
of autumn moss and leaf-litter;
they arc across wooden synapses
of yellow birch
of red spruce
on mountain peaks lifted from an empty sea.

Triumphant myriads—scarlet, brass-flecked, jet-black
and muddy,
sluggish, or coursing through the boiling streams—
their slimy skins, their tiny hands
twinkle into and out of starlight,
auguring
not a millenium

but a kind of joy.

So, the "Song of Songs"

first accompanied a dance—
a dance for the corn harvest,
between runnels and bonfires,
a carefree dance
ending in cozy tents for two,
pitched with leafy twigs, and open to the sky.

The *paynim*
talked, I suppose—
in chirrups and barks, in melodic ripples,
in droning hums

on starlit nights—
their quarreling ragged
as a rough sea
pounding a worried shore.

I doubt there was much difference
between laughter and talk.
Truth sat right down with them,
out in the open, heedless and bareheaded,

not yet driven, herded,
toward heaven—and the word
of words.

Journey

Leaving the car to continue its resolute ride,
ignoring the tires' reproach, I scale
the roadsides' corrugated cliffs
and slide like a shadow up hills and down hollows,
wind like a wraith around cryptic trees,
to lie peacefully at last along the creek bed,
looking up through liquid veils at rushing skies.

How to Enter an Iceberg

Blue-green popsicle tinting your lips.
Wearing shoes of fire.
Slowly, slowly, one toe at a time.
Nonchalantly, with sangfroid—
twirling a walking stick.
Amnesiac, forgetting your name
and where you've been.
With salt on your eyelids.
Listening to the heartbeat of whales boom
through seven oceans.
In tandem or alone.
Wearing a cloak of feathers.
Backward, trustingly,
into the frozen sea.

Connections

Approaching the Sacred

In autumn, we tromp across mountains
as though we're as tall as they are—
guns on our shoulders or
slung from our hips.

In leafy jackets, we crouch behind trees
or snipe from their branches.
We wait all winter in ambush.

Come springtime, we lean over creek banks
to reach back, through willow roots
for the snapping turtle, whose jaw clamps
tight until sunset, then loosens
and lets go.

At night, we zip ourselves into caves we've made.

We're part of the landscape;
we walk through it like
trees on the move.

We're not guests in the forest—we live here.
We grow
like an omen
out of the prophetic soil.

Winter Solstice

Three deer walked out of winter's night
and onto the mountain meadow—a stag, a doe,
a fawn, freckled silver by moonlight.

Maybe the mirror—
a deer-head mirror, cut from silvered glass,
pieces of glass for its face and ears,
glass for the wide, branching horns—maybe
the mirror called them.
Maybe the tree, unlit, in the corner
with ornaments darker than the room itself.
Or the midnight puff of the heater
with its answering row of little blue fires.
Maybe the young woman
standing barefoot at the window,
looking out of the dark room,
across the frost-covered yard
and past the cut-back rose bush,
past the gray shape of the truck,
along the gravel road, and up the hill,
where leafless trees, like antlers,
wait to carry the sun.

Quickly

Today, one of the rabbits we've put on the dole
went into its trance—dark, oval eyes
unfocused but fixed
on distance.

A red-headed woodpecker
knocked, just under the eaves.

Tonight, the driveway looks white in midsummer
    moonlight;
it curves downhill
past twin Lombardy poplars, crowded now
by untamed locust trees, tattered weeds,

and scraggly daisies.

The night air is prickled,
haphazard with fire-flies;

scattered stones light the way to the forest.

I know the oak is poised to open.

Spring

I shake its baby bottle,
and the spotted fawn
comes clicking across the porch.

Summer

The woodpecker taps news
of good fortune.

Fall

Daintily out of the mud,
a mastiff perches
on his doghouse roof.

Winter

Moving van packed,
we rest on the porch.
A whipporwill calls.

Duality

Burial Ground

Eating the hearts of our old enemies
we name our trucks, our teams,
our cities. In hope of courage
we conjure the painted warriors.
But their spirit's not sleeping in language—
our words can't call them.

In the silence of pine trees,
in the heart of the wind,
at the breathless height of the falcon
hanging before she stoops,
the warrior spirit smolders,
like fire in the camas' dark bulb.

Isleta Pueblo

Our black pick-up truck
prowls over the horizon
in another little invasion.

Noon in the pueblo
the sun gives no quarter, not even a shadow.

*Avenyu, the water serpent
has crawled away into the desert.*

Softness looks forsworn,
except in the curve of the adobe ovens
beside the ochre cubes
of adobe homes, circles and squares,
arc and line, like pottery
preserving the spirit—

clay rubbed smooth,
baked.

He has left these feathers behind.

Bisected and pressed hard
by the wheel,
this place says no.
Only the quiet—quick or slow—
cam grow here.

Sculpting the Air

On our primeval planet,
the air was pressed into place by flowers
--the fern curled the sky around it;
trees tunneled upward and out—
etching one Spring onto another.

Creatures nudged in, notching the air
with fins and noses, opening sculpture
that closed behind them;
a broad scallop behind the elephant's ear,
an invisible fan around the peacock's tale.
Then homo faber, the maker, forged new shapes
in the air. Sails cut slits opening the world.
Cities appeared, dissecting the sky.
Cinders pocked the dome overhead.

Sculptors, some say, must free the figure—
force imposed cracks the wood.
What is the figure the earth offers to us?
What is the beauty that resists our will?

Reptilian Brain

The mystics were right—
a serpent sleeps in the human brain,
its head buried in the soft flesh of memory.
Sleeping in blood
its fangs drip primeval dreams,
and its tail
threads desire
through the beads
of our spine.

Something like Enlightenment

The snow crane's
white feathers dance—
on the lake's frozen no.

Spring fog hides the ground and the sky.
Only the trees have much to say.

Wings spread, a crane
flies above the skylight
below the summer clouds.

At the edge of the lake,
the long-legged crane.
Yellow mountains behind him and in the water.

Mother

Every time we see a deer at the edge of the woods,
Mother, filled with delight,
offers a kind of prayer: "Thank you, deer,
for letting me see you."

As we walk from the house to the car,
we hear birds tweeting,
and she asks,
"Do you hear? They're talking to us."

Duality

Haunting

Like the screeching of an owl—
now here, there now;
like the white of fallen snow—
winds stop, winds blow;
as a gate to empty fields
never gives, never yields,
so the spirit takes its form
from each thing that calls it home.

Fragment

Rather a piece of bone
or shell, pierced
and threaded,
fitting my palm.

Rather a bowl, buried
alongside me
or handed, as I
pass, to son
or daughter.

All of earth or bone
or marrow, all
of leaf
and ash.

Fingerprints

Identity is distance between ridges,
location of the delta, loop, and core:

two innermost lines
begin in parallel, then diverge
to surround the pattern—
        plain whorl
        or tent loop—
each concentric whirlpool
flowing toward the center
or drifting to the edge

making a world of inside and out
as we all do
starting out as rain
ending up as snow.

Barbara Sabol

Barbara Sabol's writing is inspired by the landscape, from the mountains of western Pennsylvania where she was raised amidst the coal and steel country. She now lives in Akron, Ohio near the Cuyahoga Valley National Park whose trails she knows by heart.

Barbara was named co-Ohio Poet of the Year for her book, *WATERMARK: Poems of the Great Johnstown Flood of 1889* (Alternating Current Press, 2023.) She writes both traditional long-form and short-form poetry. Her collected haiku is part of a combined book with Larry Smith titled *Connections: Morning Dew: Tanka by Larry Smith and core & all: haiku and senryu* (Bottom Dog Press, 2022.) Barbara's chapbook, Mapping the Borderlands: haibun and tanka prose, is forthcoming from Sheila-Na-Gig Editions. She is a retired speech therapist who lives with her bird carver husband and wonder dog.

Beholding the Mountains: the poet's "i"

Reading and practicing haiku for the past 15 years has further deepened my attention to the natural world—from back yard birds and blossoms to the forests and rivers in our neck of Northern Appalachia. Heightened attention garners an awareness of a spotlit now, of being fully present. As the poet's focus moves beyond the self, the poem's

"I" becomes an "i." Momentarily detached from ego, the human observer is of no greater rank than dragonfly, branch, stream.

Appalachian poetry also reflects a strong connection with nature, with the self downsized in proportion to the surrounding landscape. I think of classic Asian painting, where mountain peaks loom large over the small figures of fishermen and villagers, making them appear incidental to the landscape's majesty, but at the same time part of the narrative.

An added feature of Appalachian literature is family and roots: how one's people have worked the land and lived in relationship to it. The writer carries on and honors that tradition. This perspective also establishes a "part of something larger" view, the poet preserving their heritage and speaking for the landscape that continues to shape us.

Sliding the Boat Back In

It returns to me in flashes, surfacing like fragments of a dream—glint of light off the water; that pungent mineral scent; a soft plash under my paddle, occasional bird song. Those free-flowing years

I lived in the bottom half of an old hunting lodge on 32 wooded acres, a private refuge set back from a busy road. Turning down that long gravel drive after work, my muscles softened, breathing deepened.

Tinker's Creek cut through the propety, attracting furred and feathered company: heron, deer, beaver, muskrat. I'd change from business clothes into jeans, hoist my blue poke boat over one shoulder, paddle over the other, and head down to the water. My life then as elementary as that clear-running creek.

wending my way
back home...
the scenic route

Return
    after Liu Tsung-Yuan

A trace of steam lingers above the kettle as she steeps
her tea in the straw-colored light filtered through the
    blinds.
Just past dawn, she leaves the house, crosses the
    western
meadow, carrying nothing. She grows smaller as the
    land
slopes to the river. Shield your eyes against the sun—
golden balls of light that settle in heron nests high
in the sycamore, and she is gone.

Listen: scuff of a wooden hull over the pebbled bank—
she rows out with the current, scattering clouds that
    float
in the water.

Given Back

The sun pale this late autumn afternoon, as though filtered through gauze. Tea-stained tints of meadow grass and sedge border the path. Now and then, I run my fingers through rushes, silky as a child's hair. The land has been given back to itself—returned to its instinctive sprawl, its mossy, hummocked earth, its vernal pools. Winterberries in the low shrubs, cardinals dotting the sycamores—vivid against this faded autumn palette.

century home wallpaper
under the heirloom roses
more roses

The sharp-toothed gears of the wetland have paused. Its industry now is shelter—the pond snail burrows into soft earth, closes her door to the coming cold; garter snakes twine in their hibernaculum. Still, dormant life hums under my tread, like a promise. Nothing, nothing but nature fanning out, digging in, cycling into what comes next.

snow-bound frog and i suspend the heart's rhythm.

Haiku

wetland walk
even my sins
cleansed

*

wild blueberries
the forgotten taste
of Eden

*

wick centered
in warm beeswax
autumn equinox

Ode to Spring, Peeper

After your frozen sleep, dreams of beetles,
of robin song, of mud-sweet air, of what passes
for love at the wetland's edge, your heart resumes
its lusty rhythm, and you rustle awake in your snug
of last autumn's leaves.

Small as a child's thumb, piercing as a night train,
you stir the woods back to what you sing for
 —another spring. So begins the forest song.

Elsewhere, ice caps weep into the sea; waters warm
and rise. Yet here, this enormous chorus, a halleluiah
of miniature bells, beckons me out to the moon-struck
      yard.

Summer Along the Stonycreek

From a needle eye in the Alleghenies
this sheet of liquid shimmer
unseams the earth.

Steel rail and forest trail
run alongside, north and west
to the Laurel Highlands. At this bend
the current circles, chisels, deepens

for the child's cannonball,
the raccoon's cupped hands,
ribbon snake's undulations,
a polished assembly of stars.

See how the water gathers
oak's shadow, hemlock's needled brush
in its wending,

how the shifting clouds and lift
of broad-winged hawk echo
on its surface.

One with sky, river meets itself
as deluge, thin rain, as mist.

A body could float through time
on its muscled back. Our stories
are ferried in its depths: caravan
of arrowhead, latchkey, crockery, bone.

Listen now to the river's patter, reminding us
Not everything is broken.

(final italicized line from "High Desert, New Mexico"
by Kim Addonizio)

Haiku

sweetgrass tips
toward the shaded bench
come, sit

*

the way she moves the earth cloud hands

*

moon flower
the night garden
fragrant with light

The Wild Wood

Mid-winter darkness is already falling as I trek through a foot of new snow, searching for my dog, Lumi. Venturing off-trail through the woods, I hold out my lantern, the only source of light this moonless night. The park ranger says, "Coyotes probably got her." I'd rather imagine that she has entered an enchanted kingdom where a rabbit, seeing that she is lost, snuggles her in its burrow or that she has found shelter in the bole of a tree.

hobo spider
i too
spin my web

This morning, a call from a hiker who spotted a dog matching Lumi's missing dog picture. I drive to the edge of the park, miles from where I lost her three days ago. Atop a steep hill that arches down to the river, I call her, long and loud, the way my mother would sing my name when the street lights came on. A form takes shape at the bottom of the hill—a snow swirl or my small, white dog?
Rib-thin, mud-slushed, exhausted, she comes limping toward me. I scoop her up, cradle her under my jacket and together we bow to the benevolent mysteries that move through the forest.

second bloom
frost flowers
glaze the field

Haiku

singing bowl
the owl's
round note

    *

        quiet
        until the doe's ear
        pivots

            *

                smoke screen
                the stories we tell
                around the fire

Fishing the Stonycreek
            —Decoration Day, May 30, 1889

Hip-high in this cold mountain creek, alone
with my own good company. That's all I require.
Nothing but the current ripple, chickadees calling
back and forth from the hemlocks. My casting rod
and a pocket-full of spinners and craw jigs.

Here, I'm delivered from the never-ending drone
of the saw blade cutting through the pine. White pine,
tall and straight as any man could hope
to carry himself.

Sun's high, glittering the water and baking the nip
out of my bones. Nothing but chill rain here lately.

Let everyone and their uncle crowd into town
for the parade, and cheer for their reed bands
and wagons full of old Union soldiers.

Give me solitude and smallmouth bass swirling
in the bug bait. Water's high as ever I've seen it.
After all these days of rain the current's swift,
      whipped up
with eddies. My read is to cast out long to the cobbled
      bank,
then walk it down the shoal.

I could plant myself in this creek for hours, breathing in
that sweet mineral water and pine sap, the sun warm
on my neck. Easy enough to hold still and wait.
      In time,
the bass will leap. There! A gold dorsal fin rising
to the surface. A quick snap on the line and now
it's just that fish and me and this mountain stream.

Haiku

break shot starlings burst from the field

          *

        dwindling days. . .
        geese carve a vee
        in the evening sky

          *

                after the harvest
                grasshopper rasp
                deep in the chaff

Song of Wood

In the pitch only dogs can hear before a quake,
my grandfather's oak rocker spoke like the rumble
of the tracks two towns down the line.

In harmony with the clatter of the coal furnace,
another double at the ironworks, it rasped a requiem
Sanctus, Sanctus, for each of the five babies whisked

by fever or fairies (*hush now*) into the Allegheny hills,
a lullaby for the eight others who lit candles
for their fledgling souls.

In a dialect of coke and ash, snuff and sweat,
it kept time with the ordered prosody of the clock.
Its scarred arms absorbed his torments, attended

the penance of ten rosaries recited into dawn.
Hail Mary, full of grace. After so many tears flooded
his stubborn lungs, it rocked him, rocked him.

He donned his serious brown suit, called us, asked
     Please,
take me to Mercy. Later that rocker fell into a heap
of spindles and posts; now our broken lament.

Blessed are we, who mourn

The Art of Stacking Wood

Hands bunched in our pockets, we stood
for minutes that fell like rain, figuring
how to build a frame for the unruly
pile of firewood, half-green, on my drive.

My father circled the cord of logs
plunked in a great heap. Old bones.
His torso bowed against the late autumn wind,
smooth as a whetted blade through smoke.

Splintered fence posts, broken-off chair legs
served as rails, milk crates as pallets.
He measured and nailed with a precision
that seemed extravagant for firewood,

then showed me how to lay the logs
crisscross for air, stability. Piston-steady,
he hoisted, I stacked, straightening the layers
as they rose, on into evening, as if practiced.

Late then, not quite dark, he butted his palm
counter to the end rounds, leveling our tower
of latent warmth, then rested his hand
on my shoulder, and we went in for supper.

Waterwheel
—Johnstown, PA. July 19, 1977

I heard my father's story a full two days later
after frantic calls home. All wires down.
Red Cross lines besieged. Try again later. . .
    later.

On his way to work at the mill that morning
my father's car headed down into the city
as the flood rose to meet him, rising fast, up

the steep road so that he threw the car into reverse
and sped some one thousand feet back up that incline,
shimmying curb-to-curb all the way to the house

on Bluff Street where he woke my mother, and together
they ran to the corner, Mom still in her bathrobe, to
        witness
the neighborhood below become a fast-running creek.

From a collision of thunder up near Erie, a series
of storms had followed one another like train cars
on a track moving down to the Conemaugh Valley,

opening their colossal cargo of rain over our town,
bursting dams built to check the river, washing away
houses, lives. Seventy-eight souls.

Through the years he'd tell it exactly the same way,
like a passage he'd memorized for school, with
the same wide-eyed astonishment as if he were

once again watching that torrent rush toward him—
trapped behind the wheel with no option but to
        hightail it
backward to higher ground.

Through the years I'd ask, *tell me again, Dad, how
you escaped the flood that day*, and silently recite
the story along with him, like a prayer,

together we'd see the sky as a sheet of molten steel,
and the marvel of that surging tide.

Kind of Blue

mill town
somewhere in the sooty sky
stars   stars
       stars

appalachia—
the abandoned quarry
our Riviera

laundry day—
a queue of blue collars
pinned to the line

picture window
the view beyond
these hogback ridges

autumn blaze
this fire
in my belly

**Why Our Mothers Warned Us About Playing
in the Creek**

It was less about jagged tin lids, or the mossy slickness of
    rocks
tumbled down from the hillside than bigger dangers our
    mothers
couldn't name. More about what was hatching beneath
    those rocks.
A quickening. Larvae set to emerge as nimble-legged,
    winged creatures.
The instinct to course into larger bodies of water. Or vanish
into air.

that first puff
of a cigarette. . .
fading contrails

Imperative

This morning on your drive to work, watch
for the weathered red canoe at the bend
of Killian Road. Slow down when it appears—
edged now by a dreary heap of snow, cocked
against a greening willow that pins the curve
of land banking the Cuyahoga. Prow points
to the water, fixed mark against a delirium
of thawing river.

Pull to the berm (today, when the warming air
is a hand on the small of your back). Cut
the engine and walk down to the water,
leaving behind briefcase, keys, shoes. Undo
the frost-slicked slip-knot and, wet to the knees,
guide the boat past the river's lip. Part the clouds.
Glide. Mind only current, eddies, the drift.

Haiku

curving
with this creek
the heron's neck

      *

                    doing nothing
                    doing everything
                    side porch breezeway

                          *

                              wind in the sweetgum
                              sun-yellow stars
                              fallin
                                    g

Happiness

The mouth
of the vase
is not calling out

for asters,
for water
its cobalt glass

curves
around the notion
of flowers

a quenched stem
and window light
scattering

the blueness.

Distant Harvest

At the vintage farm I bow into the smithy's grey and white interior, hazy in the low light. The farrier's rasp and snippers rest on the rough stone block by the firepot, long cooled. Still, I hold my hand over it, half expecting heat.

in the sooty shed
Pop's wooden chisel
hangs on a peg—
all the skills
I never grasped

*

perfectly seasoned
cabbage soup—
mom's wooden spoon

*

community garden
so many names
for lettuce

Barbara Sabol's Acknowledgments
Grateful acknowledgment to the editors of the journals, anthologies and books in which these poems first appeared:

Connections: core & all—haiku and senryu: "Kind of Blue"; *Drifting Sands Haibun*: "The Wild Wood"; *Embracing Wetlands*: "Given Back"; *I Thought I Heard a Cardinal Sing— Ohio's Appalachian Voices*: "Summer Along the Stonycreek"; *Impost—A Journal of Creative and Critical Work*: "Fishing the Stonycreek"; *McQueens Quinterly:* "Distant Harvest"; *Modern Haiku*: "Why Our Mothers Warned Us About Playing in the Creek"; *Original Ruse*: "Happiness"; *Solitary Spin*: "Return," "Imperative"; *Songs for Wild Ohio*: "Ode to Spring, Peeper"; *The Distance Between Blues*: "Song of Wood," "The Art of Stacking Wood"; *Women Speak—Women of Appalachia Anthology*: "Waterwheel."
Many thanks also to the editors of the haiku journals where the haiku were first published: *Acorn; Brass Bell; Haiku Netra; Kingfisher, Shadow Pond Journal; tsuri-dōrō*

Timothy J. Russell

Timothy J. Russell (1951-2021) was raised in Follansbee, West Virginia, and spent his adult life along the Ohio River in Toronto, Ohio. He was retired from the Weirton Steel Corp. where he worked as a boiler repairman. It was in the mill that he earned the nickname 'Mad Dog' by co-workers and 'Steel Mill Poet' fondly by fellow writers, including Jim Daniels, Frank Lehner, Marc Harshman, Richard Hague, Valerie Newman, Maggie Anderon. Many of his daily happenings at the steel mill were shared in his poems as well as his experiences in nature.

Tim was a veteran of the US Army (Sgt.) having served during the Vietnam Era as a Military Police Sentry Dog Handler from 1970-1972. He graduated from Madonna High School (1969) in Weirton, then earned a Bachelor's degree from West Liberty College (1977) and a Master's degree in Creative Writing from the University of Pittsburgh (1979).

As his wife, Jodi recalls, "Tim tended to his gardens along the Ohio riverbank and built a stone henge fondly called 'Tim Henge' across from his house. He grew poppies, zinnias, and sunflowers in it throughout the years. Battling knotweed on the river hillside he created a bird and wildlife sanctuary ever mindful of sharing and taking care of the earth for everyone and everything."

He was the author chapbooks: *The Possibility of Turning to Salt* 1987 which received the Golden Webb Award, 1987; *In Dubio* 1988; *In Medias Res*, 1991. In 1993 he received the Terrence des Pres Prizeia Poetry (Tri Quarterly Books) for his first full length book, *Adversaria*, 1993. In later years he authored chapbooks: *What We Don't Know Hurts*, 1995, and *In Lacrimae*, 1997. In 1999 he received 4th Shiki International Haiku award Shiki team which included a trip to Japan. His *In Plena Vita: The Full Life: Collected Poems* appeared in 2023 from Bottom Dog Press.

His last haiku, written, a few days before he died:
Snoozles
The little dog knows
I'm toast – 9/13/21

Working-Class Zen

That play between Nature and industry was unavoidable for me. That's the way my world appears. And, if I'm just taking objective notes without any value judgment, then half of the things I write about are going to be industry, and roughly half are going to be natural, because that's what I see when I walk out the door.

Yes, nature is a presence, a comfort...but the natural world in my mind is closer to my home. I mean that's where the poppies grow and that's where I see the orioles. I don't see them flying through the mill...so that's where the comfort of nature is; it's being home and comfortable and safe. And for that half of my life in the mill those natural things are rarely there...except maybe the deer walking on the island.

People I work with have lives outside of the mill. The same way I spend my time writing poetry, some of them run bars, tend farms...they have lives, they're people.

(from *The Writers Forum* video interview with Stan Rubin, 1995)

The Margin for Error

The scenery here is unimpressive. Mud
under the catalpa
or the sycamore is gray
as an old snow tread
abandoned for years in somebody's garage, useless.
This is a region
where everything is inexact,
where nothing matters
where it takes rain
to suppress the smell of creosote.
Geographically
the margin for error is bounded
on all sides
yet almost coincides with tolerance,
the way a confused system of roots
will fill the clay pot.

Vigilance

The swing creaks under me, although I'm still.
My knee warns me before every storm,
and it's easy to say the flickering there is
lightning or the same strain the swing
resents, but impossible to recall now that fury
is gone, the thunder, distant the lightning
occasional, the rain remains streaming on the
pavement,

and I know swirling in the downspout.
I wonder how long all this water will
take by its undeniable logic to find the
Ohio.

A small plane escaping the storm approaches,
and if the pilot were anybody but some Bogart,
I'd want to talk him safely down.

The engine falters but resumes its rhythmic stutter.
Bogie bound for the west unaware,
I'm here watching, not even a blip on his screen,
thinking the whole time he passes overhead
something is on the verge of finally happening.
Once I would've said give me enough kindling
and I'll set the world on fire,
but bravado recedes like so much thunder.
I'm only a man sitting on a porch swing
waiting and listening for something.

Even If It's Wrong

A man gets to thinking when he
spends too much time out in the sun
watching everything he knows,
his family and the place he loves,
slowly getting all the juice baked out of it
and he gets hold of something
when he's concentrating on how thirsty he is
and how afraid as his eyesight dries up, and how
he mourns the loss of sweat, and how he knows
the stones and few trees are all cooking and
heated through to their hearts, and how he would
 give anything he has to have all the water he
could ask for,

anything to be caught in the rain,
and how everyone he knows is praying for it,
and how he wonders why his God would do
this, and he decides he's not going to sit idle but
he's going to pick up a hammer
and do something in preparation.
Now I don't know that it's going to rain,

but I believe it will, and I believe
that when it finally does, it won't
stop, not for a good long while.
Nobody knows what's going to happen,
but it stands to reason
something will.

Steel Mill Ornithology

As far as we know, here
no crane normally wades
among reeds in shallow water.
As far as we know,
there are just four species:
bridge, gantry, jib, and mobile,
all most commonly safety yellow,
all intelligent creatures,
able to dip, swivel, pivot, and glide,
while hoisting several times
their own considerable weight.
One subspecies of the mobile,
smaller and more agile,
is popularly called a cherrypicker.
Most cranes are extremely responsive
to humans.
As far as we know,
there is no such thing
as a whooping crane.

Small Wonder

The sky has no color now
that the streetlights are on.
If I were twenty years younger,
the mercury vapor would be incandescent,
and I would have to be
home by now
and probably sweating in bed
contending with starved
mosquitoes, but I'm on the back porch
watching robins come down to the yard
to feed, and the fireflies signaling,
one climbing the tulip tree,
a cat moving slowly across the
yard, and the robins dispersing.
I smell rain moments before
an extremely brief shower arrives.
The streetlights cast their shadows, and the
shadows gain definition. A man I don't know,
wearing a pale green jacket,
walks by in the alley.
Moths gather at the streetlights
to commit their nightly error.
A breeze alters the elms
slightly, and robins stop calling.
Nothing will undoubtedly repeat itself.

In Loco Citato

Deer still on the island venture
onto the slag perimeter road
to feed on corn thrown down
by the payloader operator.
The deer are not cunning.
This is simply the way it is
between them. I understand
this is not an experiment.

The spotlight of a tug
shoving barges upstream
sweeps the river
catches for an instant
a few deer on the island feeding
one or two of them looking up.
The light veers from bank to bank
but always returns to the herd
as if whoever is at the light
doubts the deer exist.
The boat moves one way.
The river flows the other.
The deer continue feeding.
This is simply the way it is.

The operator knows deer
linger on the island.
He drops corn for them
or apples or whatever he has.
He sees the yellow deck-lights
of tugs on the river. At night
he loads conveyors with coke.
Although he works alone
building the huge coke piles
he is not lonely. He sees
the beam sweeping back and forth
across the river. He sees it stop.
Deer still on the island venture

onto the slag perimeter road
to feed on ears of corn. Sometimes
truck drivers from the mainland plant
cross the bridge to the island
hoping to see a few deer.
A truck crosses the bridge

moves along the idle battery
past the quencher that never really worked
past the empty and quiet payloader
past the inclined conveyors.
The truck stops long enough
for a passenger to get out.
I have to bleed the propane
from a defective cylinder.
I walk over to the river.
A tire floats downstream.
The river is high and muddy.
I wonder how fresh the deer tracks are—
have barely enough time to look up—
and see five or six deer stumbling
through the brush. Later
with propane still leaking
I find corncobs on the slag road.

Jade Plant

Some days I think it must be a green chorus of
    voices
joined in a silent medley of anguish you can
    almost see.
Every week there's ignore. Or is it somehow
    rejoicing?

Some days the plant is an ideal audience, or sentry,
listening in all directions for the smallest hint of
    truth,
or relief. I know it suffers more than a little

too much water sometimes, not enough at others,
but the brown scaly patches are symptomatic of
    nothing
more than maturity. Despite the uncertainty,

another pair of pale and shiny ears, or mouths
has sprouted lately. Some days the plant is a gossip,
some days, an arthritic penitent with nothing to
    confess

but swollen with the need for discussing it anyway.
Some days this guardian at the window
whispering instructions to itself just waits,

succulent and tender as the idea of an undeclared
    lover.

Pigeon

Thirteen shades of gray,
including dove, including pearl,

an iridescent neck,
orange claws, orange beak,

obsidian eye
more than the sum of your parts

stoic on your filthy pedestal
at the end of the Open Hearth,

like some dim-witted sentry,
posted to be seen,

your belly full of corn
laced with hallucinogens.

Quit looking at me.
Don't you know it's quitting time?

Nothing More, Nothing Less

I am out here in the fog
before the sun comes up,
watching the river glide,
taking a while to decide
if the river is not, in fact,
flowing, or slipping past,
or sliding, but gliding,
slow and unwrinkled
beneath the fog it's been
giving up all night.

I am out here in the fog,
scared to death of dying
inadvertently, by my own hand,
listening to a shrill jay
and invisible mill traffic
speeding on the river road.
Slowly twirling eddies of mist
rise from the warm, or cool,
I cannot decide which, dark
olive, seductive river.

I am out here in the fog.
I am out here waiting.

Don't Get Up

Another overloaded train
drags itself, screeching
and moaning through town
as if pain could build
character after all.
Some of the maroon cars
have messages scrawled on them,

but we've seen them all before
and don't get up.
Tangled in our bedclothes,
we embrace each other,
waiting for the blasts
before the last crossing,
and it's over before we know it.

The Mechanic

Before his ruined fingers
even find the latch
he already has an idea
about what is wrong.
He has listened
and will not be surprised
when the hood rises.
He has seen every state
an engine can be in.
At night he has seen
tiny blue lightning
snapping around like
neural messages in a brain.
He can dismantle an engine
and reassemble it
without destroying it,
something no poet can do.
He knows about the hot sex
of pistons and cylinders,
how they fit together.
He knows no engine
is ever perfect,
so fine-tunes compulsively.

When he talks about lifters
and rods and bearings
and plugs and valves,
it sounds like jargon,
but it could be incantation.
He is part magician

In Varia Lectio

I am the doomed chicory
beneath the yellow sign
at the corner of the lot.
I am the black black crow
hopping about in the shade.
I am the plantain the silver
groundhog nibbles at dusk.
I am the silver groundhog.
I am the ruby-throated
hummingbird pulling up short
to examine one of the stars
in the sopping flag.
I am the blonde woman
in the little red car
fixing her bra strap.
I am the yowling catbird.
I am the full moon
glowing behind the trees.
I am the pale petunias.
I am the lightning bug
caught in the spider web,
who still blinks.
I am the Norway maple
infested with carpenter ants.
I am the poison ivy
growing in the hedge.
I am the hedge.
I am the doomed chicory.

Tim's Haiku

we stop hammering
but the echoes continue...
geese in the fall sky

first light—
a new batch of mushrooms
on the funeral home lawn

in the time it took
to go inside for iced tea...
the primrose opened

summer evening—
the balcony spider
abides my presence

monarch butterfly
on the painted iris stem
in the waiting room

behind the hay rake
chattering across the field
so many swallows

summer evening—
the balcony spider
abides my presence

fog mixed with rain
how black are the fenceposts
how green the alfalfa

Larry Smith

Larry Smith grew up along the Ohio River in the steel mill town of Mingo Junction. He worked as a newspaper boy, cook, steel mill worker, then taught high school English in Euclid, Ohio. His education came from Muskingum College, then Kent State University. For 35 years he taught writing and film at the Firelands College of Bowling Green State University in Huron, Ohio, where he and his wife Ann, a nursing professor, raised three children.

He is the author of 8 previous books of poetry, 5 books of fiction, 2 literary biographies, and 2 books of Chinese Zen poetry translation. He wrote and co-produced documentary films on authors James Wright and Kenneth Patchen. In 1985 he and David Shevin co-founded Bottom Dog Press which has edited and published 220 books of fiction, poetry, and memoir. He has directed the Firelands Writing Center for 40 years.

In 1980-1981 the Smith family lived in Sicily where he taught Beat literature as a Fulbright Lecturer. He and Ray McNiece co-edited *America Zen: A Gathering of Contemporary Zen Poets*.

In 1990 Smith studied haiku and tanka with Clark Strand at Mount Tremper Zen Monastery near Woodstock, NY, and he has attended Blue Cliff Retreats with Thich Nhat Hahn. He and his wife were cofounders of Converging Paths Meditation Center in Sandusky and Huron, Ohio.

Everyday Zen: A Statement

Let me tell you about lower case zen.

My wife's Grandma Ferroni, yes, a short rounded Italian woman with a loving face, once taught me zen, though she didn't know it. After our pasta and table talk, we gathered around the old black and white television to watch "Perry Mason," one of her favorites. When the trial got tight I jested, "Hey, Grandma, do you think he'll win this one?" She turned to me quick, eye to eye and said, "TV, it's all a bullshit! Don't you know a that?" We all laughed sitting amidst her statued saints, but I knew a zen slap when it came.

My father worked the same way, wisdom with the fewest words possible. He was a real haiku master of the working man. "Let the shovel/ throw the dirt. . . . Let the hammer/ drive the nail." What I'm getting at here is how wisdom lies all around us, that light that is everywhere. It's not academic or philosophical, but the here and now, as practical and real as a crescent wrench in your hand or a cast iron skillet on the stove, or the light on a field or river. Zen adage: "It's not what you see but how."

Years ago I wrote a long article on "Working-Class Zen" connecting Zen with the ancient Chinese Zen poets and modern teachers like Thich Nhat Hanh and Shrynu Suziki. I sent it to the big Buddhist magazines and finally they said they liked it, but...it wasn't Zen enough. I wondered if they had read poets like Wang Wei or Taigu Ryokan, or Lao Tzu. Ultimately I chalked it up to "not what you see but how," and shared it elsewhere. So another aspect of the zen spirit is to act like bamboo and bend rather than break. Appalachians have been doing that for a long time, but they don't break.

That is what I'm getting at. Whether you call it Zen or Tao or mysticism, grace, or spirit, it comes down to how you see and live your life. An open, full and loving acceptance is the Way allowing for awe and connection. And that includes the foothills of Appalachia as well as your particular space here and now. May such writing thrive and persist like bamboo in wind.

My Hut

>by Taigu Ryokan (c. 1800)
>(Translated by Larry Smith
>from John Stevens)

My hut lies in the midst of a dense woods.
Each year the spring ivy grows longer.
No news of the affairs of men.
only the song of the woodcutter.

When the sun comes up, I mend my robes.
When the moon comes out, I read Buddhist poems.
My friends, I have nothing to report.

If you would find the Way,
stop chasing after so many things.

Things My Father Taught Me

Wakened by his footsteps
as he dressed in morning dark,
I'd lie there awaiting his
call to rise and shine.

He moved with purpose
like the railroad. His hands
wore the callouses of work;
his eyes were dark pools of trust.

He taught with what he was,
with words like apples
sweet and tart—
> Trust the road
> that takes you.
> Let the saw
> do its work.

> The worst fear
> is fear of work.
> Let the shovel
> throw the dirt.

> Enjoy the work you do
> and the job will answer back.
> Let the hammer
> drive the nail.

Drawn down into his basement
where our hair was cut,
my brother and I sat
'round his heavy workbench
awaiting his words of manhood.
We grinned to see him blush,

look away to drills and saws.
Yet he spoke simply from his life:
> Women are there
> to be cared for.
> Love them as yourself.
>
> The wrong you make
> goes on until you claim it.
> Family blood extends to everyone.
> When you speak ill of another
> you speak ill of yourself.

And from the father who
never struck me, who seldom touched me,
whose knuckles were Boy Scout knots,
whose muscled arms were tools—

> When you begin to lie
> you start to sell yourself.
> Don't confuse your wants
> with your needs.
> Hold the word that hurts.
> Kindness speaks through silence.

This year I wear his hat,
feel his touch inside his coat.
Inside my voice he speaks of
what it means to be.
He loved with what he was.

Biking the Allegheny Trail

Night train to Cumberland,
watching landscapes glide by.
till we arrive with the sun,
mount our bikes and

head down to the trail.
My son, twenty yards ahead
I twenty behind, asking him
to lead as I did with my father.
Both of us pumping hard
in and out of time,
closing the distances.
Sunlight breaking through lush greens,
wide river flowing below;
a chipmunk darts across the trail,
a robin turns these woods to song.
Bikers without names pass by
nodding to our bikes and eyes.

Tunneling darkness through to light
we pedal steady over bridges
too high to look down, my heart
beating hard at the rescue side.
Ten miles and we rest
sweat soaking through our shirts,
we lean our smiling bikes on trees,
take our easy breath on benches.
Climbing and coasting
mostly steady pedaling in sync,
we go on without thinking
just doing what's essential.

Four days of cycling,
each a cycle of its own.
"And the wheels…go round and round…"
marrying us to the road we're on.
Then into the city traffic
walkers and bikers pass blankly.

Father and son, son and father,
we have arrived together, we have
made the trail our own.

The Letting

"Sitting alone I keep slipping away." - Han-Shan

Below soft clouds
wild geese in gray sky
call out directions.

Incense burns itself out
in scented trails of smoke

   * * *

>Train whistle at noonday,
>the dog whines and runs
>through his dreams,
>
>and I sit here measuring
>my life in breaths.

Crescents

In golden light
white egret perch in trees
along the riverbank.
Scent of pine and grass silence between us.

   * * *

>Under the willow tree,
>I read the ancient poets, watch
>incense trails caress the leaves.

Sun and shadows through deep woods,
cool spring water.

Bird Talk

The bright Cardinal
lands in bird seed, scaring
the golden finch away.

Young lettuce thin as paper
grows taller every day.

    * * *

    A blue jay sits on Buddha's head,
    another feeds on scattered seed in grass.
    Thoreau would have journaled this:

    "Ohio blue jay arrive from the South
    hungry for food and meditation."

At Dusk

Large white birds
descend into the trees
along the riverbank.

They fold their wings
and rest while we
watch and wait.

The scent of river
wafts by in silence.

"Egrets," someone says
and we all nod.

Alone together
along the riverbank.

Learning by Heart

March winds can blow it all away.
Tiny yellow coltsfoot flowers,
"mother and stepmother" they're called,
spread bright wreaths under the bird feeder
welcoming cardinals and jays,
robins, house finch, and wrens.

Fields nearby witness in infinite shades of green,
plants rising surely from spring mud.

Boat-shaped clouds sail by on their
simple mission of presence.
"We do not make weather," they bow and say,
"We simply carry it."

Too soon we arrive at the station,
and must sit there and wait,
counting minutes like our days.

Bare feet anchored in wet loam, I look out
to the mountain, think of my mother birthing me,
my father at work in the mill.
Our history buried inside us like poems
to be learned and recited.

Clouds at the End of the Street

They open to what is more, like a Snickers bar's
sweet caramel unleashed by your own hands,
the wrapper dropped to the movie house floor. And
the screen comes up in a splash of music and light,
that old lion's magic roaring in your face.

                                    Remember now
we're talking of clouds at the end of the street, that

everyday joy if only we look up. Some can be
gray and threatening like a King Kong enraged
yet exciting in their wild flash and clatter.
Change and clouds forever embrace.

Such sun-drenched layers of creamy white
are cakes to be eaten, their quiet glow,
candles at a hundred births.
So softly they glide over ridge and lake.
And we read them like music played
like art without talk, a meditation
of motion and light on the
life's ilver screen.

Sweetness

Above a steady strumming
a melody rises—
water over rocks.

And your clear soft voice
breaks my heart remembering.

      * * *

    When we make love
    we are nineteen again
    kissing what's still there.

    Bamboo in snow or sun
    bends without breaking.

Blackbird

I am the blackbird
I am your name.

The moon circles
like a wolf.

Too long we have
lain in moldy grass
pretending to sleep.

Too long we have
drunk the wind
and fed on clouds.

Time to rise up
let go the rope
of dreams.

Open our eyes
to our own hands
of transformation.

Loving Loss

Sitting at mass today,
then standing, kneeling,
standing again and
then—one of those long
deep moments when things
all come together for us.

Like the time when standing
in St. Peter's parking lot
near the funeral home,
I looked over to a column of smoke
rising from the crematorium chimney.
Life speaking to and through us.

Across from me, a fellow I know
sits alone, a widower of years.
And I swallow a breath, look over
at Ann at my side, knowing
that one day one of us
will be a widower. Clearly
I see our life ahead,
and shudder inside, breathe in
the stillness of deep pain
from loving someone so much
then letting them go.

And facing at last this pre-grief
we all carry for our world,
I bow to this life, accept this home,
and rest in evening light.

Connections

Under the willow tree,
I read the ancient poets, watch
incense trails caress the leaves.

Sun and shadows through deep woods,
cool spring water.

      * * *

      Far off a long train whistle
      reminds me of my mother
      gone now thirty years.

      Wind outside my window
      whispers and sighs.

Remembrance

Placing each stone
beside the bench where
dead friends once sat.

Wild geese overhead
echo their names.

      * * *

      The poet's ashes
      float on the river he loved
      then slowly sink.

      His words stay to embrace
      the wind, the sun, and rain.
              (for Tim Russell)

Monday Morning

Walking the dog at 8 a.m.
as clouds go gliding overhead
I pause. Memories of yesterday
rise like tv news watched late,
bits and pieces floating up
through a murky screen.

I close my eyes and wait. Let go
the need to hold it all,
trust the falling into place.

Years of meditation lead me to this:

> Let go the past.
> Why anticipate the future?
> Only this moment counts
> here and now.

The dog sleeps at my feet now,
coffee on my lips.

Doing Nothing
> "Poetry might make nothing happen."
> ~ Ross Gay

After sunrise and letting the dog out,
before the day turns to business,
I sit and write a poem of this day
and wonder again what change
a poem makes. Auden said it,
"A poem changes nothing."
I've written poems for fifty years,
enough to know what not to expect,
yet on I write.

The day is clear and warm enough, so
dressed in bright jacket, helmet, and gloves,
I roll my bike out from the garage.
Embracing the autumn cool, I glide
down lanes of houses, roads of old farms,
to the worn grassy trail with its
sweet smell of trees, light flickering
through golden red leaves,
brown birds and chipmunks,
my only company. Oh, pure
circling of pedals and wheels,
thoughts vanish in this ripeness,
this steady breath of doing.
The change I'm making is
in myself—this sweet unmaking—
the nothingness of a poem.

Walking a Field into Evening

For learned books, I read the grasses.
For reputation, a bird calls my name.
I cross a stone bridge with the pace of dusk.
At the meadow gate, six cows meditate.

For decades I ran my mind up hill and down;
now idleness tells me what is near.
An arrow of wild geese crosses the sky,
my body still, my feet firm on the ground.

We age like trees now, watch our seedlings
take wind or grow around us.
I'm going to mark my books lightly
with a pencil. When someone wants
to take my picture, I'll walk
towards them and embrace

No more arguments, just heart sense,
or talk about nothing.
Take long walks in the woods at dawn and dusk,
breathe in the damp musky air,
learn to listen before I die.

Bottom Dog Press
Working Lives Series

The Light is Everywhere: Appalachia Zen Poety. 104, $16
Mrs.Nussbaum's Monkey: Frank Lehner 120 pgs. $16
In Velevet: New & Selected Poems 1995-2024, Jeanne Bryner, 202 pgs, $18
Wanted: Good Family: A Novel, Joseph G. Anthony, 212 pgs, $17
A Wounded Snake: A Novel, Joseph G. Anthony, 264 pgs, $18
Lake Effect: Poems, Laura Treacy Bentley, 108 pgs, $14
Smoke: Poems, Jeanne Bryner, 96 pgs, $16
Eclipse: Stories, Jeanne Bryner, 150 pgs, $16
Blind Horse: Poems, Jeanne Bryner, 100 pgs, $16
Cycling Through Columbine, J.R.W. Case, 264 pgs, $18
Brown Bottle: A Novel, Sheldon Lee Compton, 160 pgs, $17
No Pets: Stories, Jim Ray Daniels, 134 pgs, $16
Story Hour & Other Stories, Robert Flanagan, 104 pgs, $15
Salvatore & Maria, Finding Paradise, Paul L. Gentile, 247 pgs, $18
Earnest Occupations, Richard Hague, 200 pgs, $18
Learning How: Stories, Tales & Yarns, Richard Hague, 206 pgs, $16
A Small Room With Trouble on My Mind and Other Stories, Michael Henson, 160 pgs, $17
Pottery Town, Karen Kotrba, 130 pgs, $16
Beautiful Rust: Poems, Ken Meisel, 96 pgs
In Plena Vita- The Full Life: The Collected Poems of Timothy Russell, 280 pgs, $20
Waiting at the Dead End Diner: Poems, Rebecca Schumejda, 204 pgs, $17
The Free Farm: A Novel, Larry Smith, 306 pgs, $17
The Long River Home: A Novel, by Larry Smith, 230 pgs $22; paper $16
Mingo Town & Memories, Larry Smith, 94 pgs, $15
Milldust and Roses: Memoirs, Larry Smith, 149 pgs, $12
Beyond Rust: Novella & Stories, Larry Smith, 156 pgs
Yeoman's Work: Poems, Garrett Stack, 92 pgs, $16
Drone String: Poems, Sherry Cook Stanforth, 92 pgs, $16
Choices: Three Novellas, Annabel Thomas, 180 pgs, $18
Country Doctor's Wife: Memoirs, Cornelia Cattell Thompson, $18
Voices From the Appalachian Coalfields, Mike Yarrow & Ruth Yarrow, Photos by Douglas Yarrow, 152 pgs, $17

Bottom Dog Press, Inc.
P.O. Box 465 /Huron, Ohio 44839
http://smithdocs.

Victor Depta

Other books by the author on the subject of mysticism.

The Silence of Blackberries
1999 0-9666608-0-3

The Simultaneous Mountain:
Essays on Poetry and Mysticism
2005 0-9768817-0-5

The Dancing Dragon Poems
2010 978-0-9768817-5-

Twofold Consciousness:
Poetry and Essays on Mysticism
2012 978-0-9768817-7-3

Letters to Buddha
2015 978-0-978817-0-7

The Strawberry Moon
2017 978-0-9861789-1-7

Eternity Is That
2021 978-0-9861789-5-5

https://blairmtp.net/

www.ingramcontent.com/pod-product-compliance
Lightning Source LLC
Chambersburg PA
CBHW021018090426
42738CB00007B/811